Hi-Lo Passages
TO BUILD
Comprehension

Grades 3–4
by Michael Priestley

New York • Toronto • London • Auckland • Sydney
Mexico City • New Delhi • Hong Kong • Buenos Aires

Teaching *Resources*

Cover design by Maria Lilja
Interior design by Creative Pages, Inc.
Interior illustrations by Nicole in den Bosch

ISBN: 0-439-54887-X

Hi-Lo Passages to Build Comprehension

Grades 3–4

Contents

A Note for Teachers

Reading is the key to learning, and today's students read materials from an ever-increasing number of sources. They must understand what they read in traditional forms of fiction and nonfiction, such as stories and textbooks. They must also comprehend newer forms of text, such as advertisements on Web sites and e-mail on the Internet. Many students can benefit from more practice in reading, but finding good examples of hi-lo texts for instruction at different grade levels can be challenging.

How to Use This Book

The main purpose of this book is to provide high-interest passages for students to read. All the passages in this book are intended to be motivating and interesting for third- and-fourth grade students, but they are written for readers one to two grade levels behind. You can find the readability score for each passage in the table of contents. (Passages were scored using the Spache scoring criteria and range in level of difficulty from 1.80 to 3.0.) These passages can be used for practice and instruction in reading, and they can be used to help prepare students for taking tests. Mostly, they can help students enjoy what they read.

This book provides 25 grade-appropriate passages in a wide variety of genres, including nonfiction articles, stories, recipes, and interviews. Passages target comprehension skills, such as making inferences or comparing and contrasting. Each passage has three or five comprehension questions based on skills. The questions are intended mainly to help students think about what they have read. (If you want to check students' responses, you may refer to the Answer Key at the back of the book.)

These questions will also help you to assess students' comprehension of the material. In addition, they will help students practice answering test questions. The types of questions include multiple-choice items and short-answer items. Some of the passages include writing prompts to elicit longer responses.

Extending Activities

For some of these passages, you may want to have students go beyond answering the questions that are provided. For example, for any given passage you could have students write a summary of the selection in their own words or rewrite the passage from a different point of view. For some pairs of texts, you might have students compare and contrast the two selections. For other passages, you might want to create writing prompts and have students write full-length essays about what they have learned. Students will benefit from reading and analyzing these passages, discussing them in class or in small groups, and writing about them in a variety of ways.

Passage 1   Story Elements

Rabbit Laughs

Long ago, there lived a rabbit. Rabbit had a field. It was filled with weeds. Rabbit wanted to plant food. So she had to get rid of the weeds.

But Rabbit was lazy. She did not want to pull up the weeds.

Rabbit thought of a plan. She got a rope. She walked to one side of the field. There she found a big hippo. "I bet I can pull harder on this rope than you!" Rabbit told Hippo. "Just hold one end. Wait until I start to pull."

Then Rabbit took the other end of the rope. She walked to the other side of the field. There she found an elephant. "I bet I can pull harder than you!" Rabbit said. "Just hold this rope until I start to pull."

Rabbit went to the middle. She gave a tug on the rope. Hippo and Elephant began to pull on each end. They pulled hard. The rope went this way and that. It cut down the weeds. Soon the weeds were gone!

Rabbit hopped over to Hippo. "Thanks!" she said. Then she hopped back to Elephant. "Thanks!" she said.

Elephant and Hippo asked, "But who is pulling the other end of the rope if you are hopping?"

How that Rabbit laughed!

1. Where does this story take place?

Ⓐ a sea

Ⓑ a mountain

Ⓒ a field

Ⓓ a zoo

2. What was Rabbit's problem?

_____

3. Which word best describes Rabbit?

Ⓐ sad   Ⓒ mad

Ⓑ helpful   Ⓓ tricky

Passage 2   Sequence

Here Comes the Sun

Do you like the sun? Here is a way to have a sun in your room every day!

You will need:

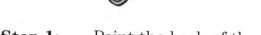

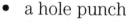

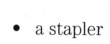

- a paper plate
- some yellow paint
- a brush
- yellow paper
- scissors

- a stapler
- a black pen
- a hole punch
- string

Step 1:   Paint the back of the plate yellow.
Step 2:   Put your hand on the yellow paper. Draw around your hand. Draw your hand 7 times.
Step 3:   Cut out the 7 hands.
Step 4:   Staple the hands to the plate.
Step 5:   Draw a happy face on your sun.
Step 6:   Make a hole at the top of the plate.
Step 7:   Put string through the hole. Hang up the plate in your room!

1. What is the first thing you should do?

_____

2. What should you do after you draw your hand 7 times?

_____

3. What is Step 6?

- Ⓐ Make a hole.
- Ⓑ Draw a happy face on your sun.
- Ⓒ Staple the hands to the plate.
- Ⓓ Cut out the 7 hands.

6

Passage 3   Story Elements

Troll's New Look

Once there was a troll who lived under a bridge. Every day he scared people. That is what his father told him to do. That is what all trolls do. Troll yelled, and people ran away.

"Good job!" said his father.

But Troll was very sad. His was a lonely job.

"No one ever talks to me. No one ever smiles," he said.

"Of course not!" said his father. "You are a troll! No one will *smile* at you."

When Troll heard this, he sat under the bridge. He thought he would never move again.

The next morning, three girls came to the bank of the river. Troll knew he should yell and wave his arms. But he wanted to smile. He wanted to tell them how pretty they looked. Then he remembered what his father had told him. He yelled.

"What was that?" screamed the big sister.

"It must be a monster!" screamed the middle sister. They both ran back the way they had come.

But the little sister looked under the bridge. She saw Troll. "Who are you?" she asked.

"I am just a troll," said Troll. "No one will ever smile at me."

"Think about how you look," said the girl.

"What do you mean?" asked Troll.

"If you sit under bridges and look wild, people will not smile at you. They will be scared of you," said the girl. "You need to change the way you look!"

"How?" asked Troll.

"You need to take a bath. Cut your hair. Wear some nice clothes!"

Troll thought hard about what the girl said. Then he took a bath in the river. After that he walked into town. First he went to a barbershop. He said, "Please cut my hair."

"As you wish, Mr. Troll," said the man.

Next Troll bought some nice clothes. He paid with some fish from the river.

"Thank you," said the man in the store, and he smiled at Troll! That made Troll smile to himself all the way home.

1. At the beginning of the story, where is Troll?

    Ⓐ under a bridge

    Ⓑ in a store

    Ⓒ in a house

    Ⓓ on an island

2. What is Troll's problem?

_____

_____

3. How does Troll solve his problem?

_____

_____

4. Where does Troll walk to near the end of the story?

_____

5. How does Troll feel at the beginning of the story, and how does he feel at the end?

_____

_____

Scholastic Teaching Resources

Grades 3-4

MEET JORGE ESTRELLA

Jorge Estrella writes for a newspaper. He works for Big Sky News. We spoke to him to find out about his job.

Question: How long have you been writing news stories?

Answer: I have been writing for two years.

Q: Why did you become a writer?

A: I have always liked to write. When I was a kid, I wrote lots of stories.

Q: So why do you only write news stories now?

A: When you write a storybook, you spend a lot of time alone. I want to have many chances to meet people and talk to them. That's why I write news, not books.

Q: How do you spend time with other people as a news writer?

A: Before I write a story, I have to get facts. I see the people who know the facts. I ask them questions. Then I go back to the building where I work. It's filled with people. The people are all working on the next day's newspaper.

Q: Do you think your job is hard?

A: Some days are harder than others. On a hard day, many things happen. That means I have to write a lot of news stories. Sometimes I even miss lunch! But at the end of a hard day, I feel good about all of my work.

Q: Do you ever write news stories about kids?

A: Sure. I am working on one right now. It's about some kids who think the city needs more soccer fields. They want to find a way to get more fields.

Q: What do you think will happen?

A: Well, many people will read my story. Maybe some of them will offer to help. If they do, that will be another story I can write.

1. *Big Sky News* is the name of a _____.

   Ⓐ newspaper

   Ⓑ mystery book

   Ⓒ song

   Ⓓ college

2. From reading this passage, what can you tell about Jorge Estrella?

   Ⓐ He likes to be alone.

   Ⓑ He likes to play soccer.

   Ⓒ He likes to write books.

   Ⓓ He likes to be around people.

3. Where do you think Jorge writes his news stories?

_____

4. What would an easy day at work be like for Jorge?

_____

_____

5. To write a story about the kids who want more soccer fields, what does Jorge need to do?

   Ⓐ Meet and talk to people.

   Ⓑ Read a soccer book.

   Ⓒ Watch the kids play soccer.

   Ⓓ Give the kids a soccer field.

10

Passage 5   Drawing Conclusions

Rules for Our School

1. **SMILE.** People catch smiles just like they catch colds! If you smile at a person, he or she will probably smile at someone else. Soon the whole school will be smiling.

2. **FIND WAYS TO HELP.** If someone falls, help that person up. If someone has a lot of books, open the door. If a friend does not understand something, help him or her.

3. **ALWAYS SAY THANK YOU.** Remember to say "Thank you" to others. The person you thank will feel good. The person will also be glad to help you the next time.

4. **NEVER PUSH.** Lots of people share our school. We share the halls. We share the water fountains. You can't always be first. So do not push! You will make others angry. You might even hurt someone. Instead, say, "You first!"

1. **Why do you think you should smile?**
   - Ⓐ It can help make others happy.
   - Ⓑ Smiles are hard to catch.
   - Ⓒ Few people know how to smile.
   - Ⓓ The school will not catch cold.

2. **What is one rule that you should NOT add to "Rules for Our School?"**
   - Ⓐ Don't push others in line.
   - Ⓑ Share with other students.
   - Ⓒ Don't help new students.
   - Ⓓ Always say "Please."

3. **What lesson did you learn from these rules?**

   _____

   _____

   Writing Prompt: Do you think these rules would be good for your school? Why or why not?

Passage 6   Main Idea and Details

Talk With Your Hands

Some people can't hear. These people have a special way of talking. They talk with their hands. This is called "signing." There are two main ways to sign. First, you can spell out each letter in a word. Here is the word *love*.

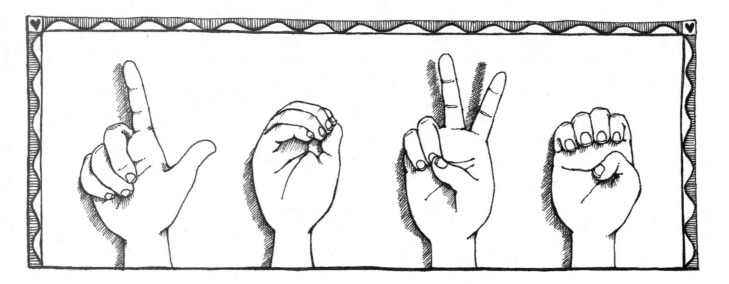

Spelling words takes a long time. There is a faster way to sign. You can show a whole word with one sign.

To sign some words, you keep your hands still. (Look at the signs for *love* and *ball* below.) To sign other words, you need to move your hands. To sign the word *dog*, you pat your leg.

Signing is lots of fun. Anyone can learn. You can learn from a book. You can learn from a teacher. You can learn from a friend who uses signing every day. Here are good signs to start with:

love

ball

hello

1. **What is this passage mostly about?**
- (A) how to be a better speller
- (B) why some people cannot hear
- (C) all the things you can do with your hands
- (D) using your hands to talk

2. **Look at the sign. What letter is it?**

- (A) L
- (B) O
- (C) V
- (D) E

3. **What word does this sign stand for?**

_____

4. **Name a word that you have to move your hands to sign.**

_____

5. **There are many ways to learn how to sign. Name two.**

_____

_____

13

Passage 7   Making Inferences and Predictions

The Right Pet

Will sat on the kitchen floor. He was holding a cookie next to a tiny hole in the wall. Will's father came into the kitchen.

"What are you doing?" he asked.

"Quiet, please," said Will. "You will scare it."

"What will I scare?" asked Will's dad.

"The mouse!" said Will. "This is a mouse hole."

"That hole does not belong to a mouse," said his dad. "I made it."

"How?" asked Will.

"I banged a chair leg into the wall. I am going to fix the hole," said his dad.

Will looked at his father. Then he looked down at the floor.

"What is wrong?" asked his father.

Will said, "Cats make Mom sick. Our apartment is too small for a dog. I thought I had found a pet at last."

His father smiled. "Wild animals do not make good pets, Will. I have a better idea. Would you like to go to the pet store?"

"Of course," Will said as he stood up. He put the cookie in his mouth. He was ready to go.

1. Why do you think Will was holding a cookie?

_____

_____

2. How do you think Will felt when he looked down at the floor?

Ⓐ happy   Ⓒ tired

Ⓑ surprised   Ⓓ sad

3. What do you think Will and his father will do next?

Ⓐ Make a hole in the wall.   Ⓒ Buy a pet mouse.

Ⓑ Get a mousetrap.   Ⓓ Make some cookies.

14

Passage 8   Sequence

Peanut Butter Fudge

Do you love peanut butter? Here is a way to make a soft peanut butter fudge. Ask an adult to help you when you use the microwave. Do not make this if you cannot eat peanuts.

A Recipe For **Peanut Butter Fudge**

YOU WILL NEED:

- 1 stick of butter
- 1 cup of peanut butter
- peanuts
- 4 cups of sugar
- $\frac{1}{2}$ cup of milk
- 1 cup of chocolate chips

- a cake pan
- a large bowl that can go in the microwave
- a big spoon
- a rolling pin
- measuring cups

Step 1: Let the butter get soft. Rub a little butter all over the sides of the cake pan.

Step 2: Put the rest of the butter in the bowl. Add the peanut butter. Put the bowl in the microwave. Put it on high for two minutes.

Step 3: Take the bowl out of the microwave. Stir well.

Step 4: Crush the peanuts into little pieces. You can do this with a rolling pin.

Step 5: Put the crushed peanuts into the bowl. Add the sugar and the milk. Add the chocolate chips. Stir everything together.

Step 6: Put the bowl back in the microwave. Turn it on high for 1 minute.

Step 7: Take the bowl out and stir well.

Step 8: Pour the fudge into the cake pan. Cool the pan for one hour.

Step 9: Cut the fudge into pieces. Eat and ENJOY!

15

1. What is the first step?

    Ⓐ Heat the peanut butter.

    Ⓑ Add the milk.

    Ⓒ Butter the pan.

    Ⓓ Stir well.

2. What do you do right before you add the peanut butter?

    Ⓐ Stir well.

    Ⓑ Put the butter in the bowl.

    Ⓒ Add milk.

    Ⓓ Add the chocolate chips.

3. What do you do in Step 4?

_____

4. What do you do in Step 7?

_____

5. What do you do just after you pour the fudge into the cake pan?

_____

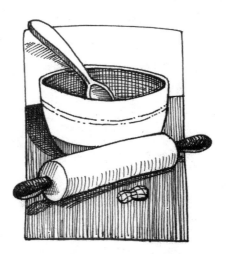

Scholastic Teaching Resources   **Grades 3–4**

Passage 9   Making Inferences and Predictions

THE SNOW PARTY

Amy and Hana woke up early on Monday. There was a loud
noise out in the street. It was the plow going by! There was snow
outside. Then there was a knock on the twins' door.

"There's no school today!" said Mom.

The girls smiled.

"Then let's go outside," they said.

After breakfast, the twins put on their snow pants and coats.

Then they went across the street to the Arnolds' house.

Amy knocked, and Mr. Arnold opened the door.

"Hi, girls," he said.

"Are you going to have a snow party today?" asked Hana.

"We always do!" said Mr. Arnold. "Go get your sleds!"

The Arnolds had a big hill behind their house. It was great for
sledding. There was just one problem. At the bottom of the hill
was a fence. If you thought you might hit the fence, you had to
roll off your sled.

Mr. Arnold went down the hill first. His sled made a safe path
through the snow.

17

Mrs. Arnold went next. She did not steer very well and had to roll off. When she came up the hill, she looked like a snow woman! The twins laughed.

Hana had a great run. She steered just right. Amy clapped.

Then it was Amy's turn. She jumped on her sled. She started down the big hill. She went so fast! The snow flew up into her face! Where was the path?

"Jump!" Mr. Arnold yelled.

Amy took a deep breath. She let go of her sled.

1. Why did Amy and Hana smile after they learned school was closed?

Ⓐ They were tired.

Ⓑ They were mad.

Ⓒ They were happy.

Ⓓ They were hungry.

2. Why did the girls laugh after Mrs. Arnold's run?

Ⓐ Mrs. Arnold looked funny.

Ⓑ Mrs. Arnold looked cold.

Ⓒ Mrs. Arnold looked scared.

Ⓓ Mrs. Arnold looked sad.

3. Why did Amy clap after Hana's run?

Ⓐ She was glad Hana had a good run.

Ⓑ She wanted to warn Hana about the fence.

Ⓒ She knew her turn would be next.

Ⓓ Her hands were cold.

4. Why did Amy take a deep breath at the end of the story?

_____

_____

5. What do you think Amy did next?

_____

_____

Passage 10   Details

Frieda and Her Trick

Frieda lives in Germany. Frieda is an octopus. Every day people come to the zoo to see Frieda. They come to see her special trick.

An octopus has eight arms. Frieda uses these arms to do her trick. She opens jars! Here is how she does it. People at the zoo put food that Frieda likes in a jar. They put the lid on tight. Then they place the jar in the water with Frieda.

This smart little octopus climbs on the jar. She holds the lid with her arms. Then she turns her body. The lid comes off!

People at the zoo think Frieda saw them open jars. Then she did it herself. Frieda only opens the jars with food that she likes!

1. **Where does Frieda live?**

   _____

2. **What is in Frieda's jars?**

   _____

3. **Frieda holds the lid with her _____.**

   Ⓐ head

   Ⓑ arms

   Ⓒ mouth

   Ⓓ tail

Passage 11   Drawing Conclusions

Creepy Spiders

Many people are a little afraid of spiders. This makes sense because some spiders can hurt people. But most spiders are safe. It is important to know that.

Ann Blaine was not just a little afraid of spiders. Every time she saw a spider, Ann screamed. She cried. She fell down. She was that scared!

If the spider was in her house, she had to leave. She would stay at a friend's house until her family caught the spider! Once she did not come home for a month!

Ann went to a doctor. Ann's doctor told her that lots of people are afraid of things. He said she could get help. He sent her to a special doctor who helps people who are afraid a lot of the time.

First, Ann had to look at pictures of spiders. To her surprise, she slowly got used to them. Next, Ann had to look at videos of spiders. Then, the doctor gave Ann's family a big, toy spider. Their job was to hide it in the house. Poor Ann! Coming across the toy spider in strange places was not fun!

Finally, the doctor said Ann was ready for a big test. He put some real spiders in front of Ann. The spiders were in jars. They were very tiny spiders. Then the spiders were let loose. Ann made herself touch one. She even let one run on her hand.

Ann is still a little afraid of spiders. But if she finds one at home, she does not have to move away for a month. She can catch the spider in a jar and put it outside—all by herself.

Scholastic Teaching Resources   **Grades 3-4**

1. **Why do you think Ann Blaine went to a special doctor?**

_____

_____

2. **Why do you think the doctor made Ann look at pictures of spiders?**

_____

_____

3. **Why do you think Ann was ready for the big test at the end of the story?**

    Ⓐ She could put spiders in jars.

    Ⓑ She could hide toy spiders in her house.

    Ⓒ She could let spiders run on her hand.

    Ⓓ She wasn't afraid of toy spiders anymore.

4. **Do you think the special doctor helped Ann? Tell why or why not.**

_____

_____

5. **Think of something else a person might be afraid of. How would you help this person if you were a doctor? How would you get the person used to the thing so it did not seem so scary?**

_____

_____

_____

_____

21

Passage 12   Cause and Effect

Asteroid Just Misses Boy!

September 1, 1991
Noblesville, Indiana —

Last night, Brodie Spaulding was standing outside his house. He heard a strange sound. Then a small rock hit the ground. It was black and brown. When Brodie touched the rock, he was surprised. The rock was warm!

Brodie's rock was very special. It came all the way from space to Brodie's yard!

Space is full of rocks. They are called asteroids. High in the air, the asteroid catches on fire. Have you ever seen a

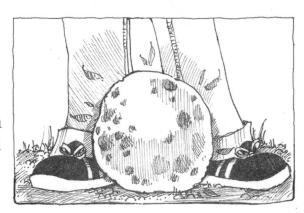

shooting star in the night sky? It is really a burning space rock. Most of these rocks burn up before they reach Earth. Only a few hit the ground.

The rock in Brodie's yard was still warm because it had just been on fire! The rock hit Earth hard because it was moving very fast. It made a hole in Brodie's yard.

Brodie felt scared. The rock almost hit him! He also felt lucky. Now he owned a space rock!

---

1. Why was Brodie surprised when he touched the rock?

   Ⓐ It was brown.   Ⓒ It was small.

   Ⓑ It was black.   Ⓓ It was warm.

2. Why did the asteroid make a hole in Brodie's yard?

_____

3. Why did Brodie feel scared about the asteroid?

_____

Passage 13   Sequence

RIDING THE BOARD

Yoko stepped on her skate board and pushed off. But this time something went wrong. Her board flew out from under her. As she started to fall, she put out her arm and fell hard on it.

Yoko rubbed her arm. She waited for the hurting to stop, but it did not. Then Yoko tried to move her arm. It hurt even more.

She looked across the park. Dad was reading a book.

She got up and she walked toward Dad. She held her arm still as she walked, but it still hurt a lot.

Now Yoko was crying. Dad moved Yoko's hurt arm just a little bit.

"Ow!" shouted Yoko. "That hurts!"

Dad took Yoko to the doctor. Dr. Rio took an X-ray of Yoko's arm. She showed it to Yoko and her dad. The X-ray showed that Yoko's arm bone was broken.

"But I was wearing my arm pads," said Yoko. "How could I break my arm?"

"You held your arm out and landed on it. That's why it broke," said Dr. Rio. "Next time hold them close to your body."

"That's an important thing to know," said Dad.

"Yes," said Dr. Rio. "We often learn best from the mistakes we make." Then she smiled at Yoko. "Now, let's put a cast on that arm of yours."

23

1. **What happened first in this story?**
   - Ⓐ Yoko's board flew out from under her.
   - Ⓑ Yoko fell on her arm.
   - Ⓒ Yoko pushed off.
   - Ⓓ Yoko stepped on her board.

2. **What did Yoko do just before she fell?**

   _____

3. **Which of these happened first?**
   - Ⓐ Dad took off Yoko's helmet and pads.
   - Ⓑ Yoko rubbed her arm and tried to move it.
   - Ⓒ Yoko got up and walked toward Dad.
   - Ⓓ Yoko started crying.

4. **What happened next after Dad brought Yoko to the doctor?**
   - Ⓐ Dad tried to move Yoko's arm.
   - Ⓑ Yoko asked, "How could I break my arm?"
   - Ⓒ Dr. Rio took an X-ray of Yoko's arm.
   - Ⓓ Yoko's arm stopped hurting so much.

5. **After Dr. Rio took an X-ray, what did she do next?**

   _____

Passage 14   Cause and Effect

The Clean-Up Team

    Mrs. Gill lived next door to Nita. Every afternoon, Mrs. Gill took a walk. She said it kept her young. Nita liked to peek out when Mrs. Gill came back. Mrs. Gill was always happy after her walk. She often showed Nita something she had found, like a bright red leaf.

    One afternoon, Mrs. Gill looked sad. Nita asked her what was wrong.

    Mrs. Gill held up a can. "I am sad about all the trash on the street," she said. "I have never seen so much trash in this neighborhood! What has happened?"

    "Mr. Trent moved," said Nita. "He used to go out each morning and pick up trash. I often saw him on my way to school."

    Mrs. Gill looked surprised. "I thought I knew everything about this neighborhood!" she said. "But you see more than I do!"

    "I wish I could do Mr. Trent's job, but my back is stiff. It's hard for me to bend over and pick things up."

    "I could do that," said Nita.

    Mrs. Gill smiled. "I will carry the trash bag! You can use my gardening gloves so your hands stay clean."

    Nita put on the gloves. She picked up pieces of paper. She picked up cans. Lots of people stopped to thank Mrs. Gill and Nita. The street looked much better when Nita and Mrs. Gill were done.

    "Thanks, Nita," said Mrs. Gill. "Let's call ourselves the clean-up team!"

1. Why did Mrs. Gill take a walk every day?

   Ⓐ She wanted to pick up litter.

   Ⓑ She wanted to talk to Mr. Trent.

   Ⓒ She wanted to feel young.

   Ⓓ She wanted to start a club.

2. Why was Mrs. Gill sad one day?

   Ⓐ She lost a red leaf.

   Ⓑ The streets were full of trash.

   Ⓒ She lost her gloves.

   Ⓓ Nita was bothering her.

3. Why did the neighborhood have so much trash?

_____

_____

4. Why did Nita pick up the trash instead of Mrs. Gill?

_____

_____

5. Why did Nita's hands stay clean?

_____

_____

26

Name _____   Date _____

Sisters in Space

Venus is close to Earth. It is the second planet from the sun. Earth is third from the sun. Venus and Earth are almost the same size. That's why Venus is called Earth's "sister planet."

Scientists have been learning about Venus for a long time. First they looked at Venus through telescopes. Telescopes make things that are far away look closer. But Venus is covered with thick clouds. The scientists could not see Venus through the clouds. So they made guesses about it.

For a long time, scientists thought that Venus had water and plants. They thought Venus might have animals, too. But they could not know for sure.

Then scientists found a way to learn more about Venus. In 1978, they began sending space probes to Venus. Probes are tools that are used to look at things. The probes flew through the thick clouds. They took pictures of Venus up close. They found out other things, too. The probes sent the pictures and things they found out back to the scientists.

The scientists learned a lot from the probes. First they learned that most of their guesses were wrong. Nothing could ever live on Venus. Why not? Venus is much, much too hot.

Venus

After that, scientists knew they could not send people to Venus. But they still wanted to know more about it. So they made new probes. These new probes took great pictures of the planet. The pictures showed that Venus has plains, mountains, and valleys. In some ways, Venus looks like Earth.

Earth

1. Why is it hard to see much of Venus through a telescope?

_____

_____

2. Why did scientists send probes to Venus in 1978?

_____

_____

3. What is the main reason people can never visit Venus?

   Ⓐ It does not have water.

   Ⓑ It is a long way from Earth.

   Ⓒ It does not have plants.

   Ⓓ It is much too hot.

4. Why did scientists send new probes to Venus?

   Ⓐ The telescopes broke.

   Ⓑ The old probes were lost in space.

   Ⓒ They wanted to know even more about Venus.

   Ⓓ They wanted to show that people could live there.

5. What new things did scientists learn because of the new probes?

_____

_____

28

Name   Date

Passage 16   Story Elements

The Very Hungry Kid

One morning a mother goat led her kids up a mountain. The mountain was tall. After walking for a while, the kids grew tired. They asked their mother to let them rest. But she told them to keep going. "I see grass just above us," she told them. "We'll be there before you know it."

Soon the goats reached the grass. "How good it tastes, Mother!" the kids said. They began to eat.

But before long, the biggest kid began to worry. "This grass is sweet," he said. "But the hard walk made us all very hungry. I am sure there is not enough grass here for all of us."

"That is silly," his mother laughed. "There is more than enough grass here."

The biggest kid did not listen to his mother. Instead he looked over at the next mountain. On it he saw a green patch. His mouth began to water. "I shall go down this mountain and up the next," said the biggest kid. "There I will have all the grass for myself."

Grades 3–4   **Scholastic Teaching Resources**

So he started off. The trip down the first mountain took a long time. The walk up the next mountain took even longer. At last the biggest kid reached the green patch he had seen from far away. But now his heart sank. Instead of grass, all he found were weeds. The weeds had a very bad taste.

The biggest goat had to go back to his family. As he made his way back, he cried. "By now my brothers and sisters have eaten every piece of grass. I am sure they have left nothing for me."

For the second time that day, the biggest kid was wrong. When he found his family again, they were sleeping in the warm sun. Most of the grass was chewed down to its roots. But there was still some grass for him. It was more than enough to fill the biggest kid's very empty belly.

1. At what time of day does the story begin?

_____

2. Where did the mother goat lead her kids?

_____

3. Why did the biggest kid go down the first mountain and up the next?

_____

_____

4. What happened when the biggest kid went up the second mountain?

_____

_____

5. Which word best describes the biggest kid?

    Ⓐ brave   Ⓒ smart

    Ⓑ scared   Ⓓ greedy

Writing Prompt: On a piece of paper, tell all the important things that happen in this story.

Passage 17   Main Idea and Details

Snow Caves

People are not made to live in very cold weather. We do not have fur to keep us warm! We must make our clothes and shelter.

In winter, you must be careful. If you get stuck outside for a long time on a cold day, you may freeze. So what can you do to stay warm?

First, find a big pile of snow. Then, dig a cave. Make the cave big enough to hold air for you to breathe. Before you climb inside, brush any snow off your clothes. The heat from your body will be trapped inside the cave. This is good! But if your clothes are snowy, the snow will melt. This is bad. Wet clothes will pull the heat right out of your body

Climb into your cave. Next, fill up the door hole with snow. This way the heat will not get out. If you can, share your cave with a friend. Two people make more heat than one person can.

1. What is this passage mostly about?

  Ⓐ how animals live in winter

  Ⓑ what to do if you are stuck outside in the cold

  Ⓒ how to build a nice house

  Ⓓ games to play in the snow during the winter

2. What should you do if your clothes are snowy?

_____

3. Why should you fill up the door hole with snow?

_____

Grades 3–4   **Scholastic Teaching Resources**

Passage 18   Sequence

Mama's Magic Trick

Rosa, Anita, and Felipe came to the kitchen for dinner.

Rosa said, "I do not like salad."

"I know that," said Mama, "but salad is what we are having."

Then Mama put some chicken on each plate.

"I don't like chicken," said Felipe.

Last, Mama gave each of them some special rice.

"That smells so good!" said Felipe.

"I want plain rice," said Anita.

Finally, Mama said, "I cook and cook, but I can never make something that all you children like."

"That would take magic," said Papa.

Mama laughed. Then she left the room. When she came back, she was wearing a pair of wings from the dress-up box. She was carrying a wand.

She pointed the wand at all three children. "Love the food!" she laughed. "Love it all!"

Rosa smiled and took a bite of salad. Anita grinned and ate some rice. Felipe even tried some chicken. Papa said Mama's magic trick worked!

1. What happened first?

_____

2. Which food did Mama serve last?

   Ⓐ salad   Ⓒ chicken

   Ⓑ rice   Ⓓ water

3. What did Mama do after she got dressed up?

_____

_____

Grades 3-4

Passage 19   Comparing and Contrasting

What is a whale?

Many people think that a whale is a kind of fish. A whale is not a fish at all. But whales and fish are much alike.

Like fish, whales spend their lives in the water. Whales and fish both have fins. They use the fins to swim. Whales often stay together in groups. These groups are called *pods*. Many kinds of fish also stay together in groups. A group of fish is called a *school*.

Whales are different from fish in an important way. A fish can breathe underwater. A whale cannot. A whale must come to the top of the water to take a breath. It takes in air through a hole on its back. A whale can hold its breath under the water for a long time. But after a while, it must come back up for more air.

If a whale is not a fish, what is it? A whale is a mammal. There are many kinds of mammals. Dogs, cats, and horses are mammals, too.

Most mammals live only on land. Some, such as beavers, live part of the time on land and part of the time in water. Besides the whale, just one other mammal—the sea cow—lives only in water.

33

Did you know that you are a mammal, too? You are more like a whale than you might think. You have hair on your body. So does a whale. Your heart has four parts. So does a whale's. Your body always stays about the same temperature. A whale's body does, too.

Of course, you are different from a whale in many ways. You don't have fins or a tail. You spend almost all your time on land. But here's something to think about the next time you go swimming. When you dive under the water and come back up for air, you are acting just like a whale!

1. How are the bodies of fish and whales alike?

_____

2. In this article, how is a *school* different from a *pod*?

_____

_____

3. How are sea cows and whales alike?

  Ⓐ They spend their lives in the water.

  Ⓑ They are kinds of fish.

  Ⓒ They can breathe under the water.

  Ⓓ They have holes in their backs.

4. How are whales like dogs, cats, and horses?

  Ⓐ All have the same shape.

  Ⓑ All stay together in groups.

  Ⓒ All are the same size.

  Ⓓ All are mammals.

5. How is your heart like a whale's heart?

_____

_____

34

Passage 20   Main Idea and Details

What Did You Say?

People use sayings every day. You may ask an unhappy friend why she's "feeling blue." If you've done only a small part of a big job, you might call it "a drop in the bucket."

These sayings don't mean exactly what the words say. But it's easy to tell why we use them. Blue is a cool, quiet color. So it's a good word for "sad." A bucket holds too many water drops to count. So just one drop is very little.

Other sayings are more difficult to understand. When you are about to go to bed, you are going to "hit the hay." This saying does not make much sense unless you know where it came from. It was first used in the 1930s. At that time, many Americans were out of work. Some went from place to place, looking for jobs. At night they were very tired. They often made a bed of hay in a field or barn. As soon as their heads "hit the hay," they fell asleep.

Here is another saying. When you are sick, you might say you are "under the weather." But why? This saying is more than 200 years old. It began in the days when many people went from place to place by boat. When the storm winds rocked the boat, people often felt sick. The boat was sailing "under the weather."

Old sayings like these can be hard for kids to understand. But new sayings come along every day. Kids often understand new sayings better than older people do. That's why your grandmother might not know what you mean when you say "chill out" or "give me five." She might think you're "off your rocker."

1. What is this article mostly about?

   Ⓐ colors   Ⓒ jobs

   Ⓑ sayings   Ⓓ boats

2. What is another good title for this article?

   Ⓐ "Feeling Blue"

   Ⓑ "People in the United States"

   Ⓒ "Old Sayings"

   Ⓓ "A Cool, Quiet Color"

3. What does "feeling blue" mean?

   Ⓐ sad   Ⓒ mad

   Ⓑ cold   Ⓓ happy

4. What does "hit the hay" mean?

_____

5. Which saying is more than 200 years old?

   Ⓐ "feeling blue"

   Ⓑ "hit the hay"

   Ⓒ "drop in the bucket"

   Ⓓ "under the weather"

Passage 21   Comparing and Contrasting

Bug Eaters

Did you know that some plants eat bugs? They do! But first the plants must catch their food.

The Venus's flytrap has little hairs on its leaves. When a bug moves against these hairs, the plant feels it. Then the leaves snap shut. The bug is trapped.

The teasel is a plant shaped like a cup. When it rains, water stays in the bottom of the cup. Bugs fall into the water. They cannot get out.

Look at the picture of the sundew plant. Do you see the long "arms"? These "arms" make sticky drops. A bug lands on the drop and gets stuck. Then the "arms" close up. They trap the bug!

The rainbow plant also traps bugs with sticky drops.

1. Which two plants have sticky drops?

_____

2. How are all these plants the same?

Ⓐ They all have hairs on their leaves.   Ⓒ They all have "arms."

Ⓑ They all trap bugs.   Ⓓ They all have drops.

3. Which plant is shaped like a cup?

_____

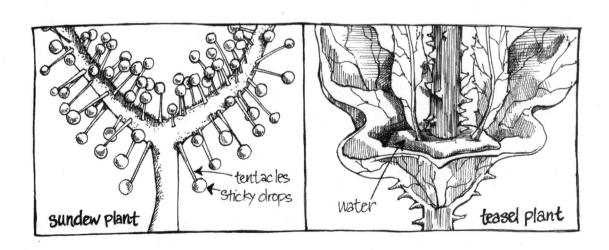

sundew plant   water   teasel plant

tentacles
sticky drops

Passage 22   Cause and Effect

A Second Chance for Seabiscuit

In 1936, a horse named Seabiscuit was put up for sale. At the age of three, Seabiscuit had run many races. But he lost most of them. His owner did not want to keep a losing horse.

A man name Charles Howard bought Seabiscuit. He had seen the horse race. He liked what he saw. Howard thought Seabiscuit could win races. He asked a man named Tom Smith to work with Seabiscuit.

Smith knew that Seabiscuit's first owner had raced him too hard. Seabiscuit was tired and mean. Smith thought that being with other animals would make Seabiscuit happy. So he put a goat next to Seabiscuit. But Seabiscuit didn't like the goat at all. He picked up the goat with his teeth and tossed it away. Next Smith put a little horse next to Seabiscuit. Seabiscuit liked the horse and began to calm down. Before long, Seabiscuit also made friends with a dog and a monkey. They were his pets.

Now Tom Smith was ready to train Seabiscuit. Smith was kind. Seabiscuit grew to like him. Soon Seabiscuit was running well. Smith told Howard the horse was ready to race again.

As Charles Howard's horse, Seabiscuit won some big races. By 1938 many people were talking about Seabiscuit. They thought he might be the best racehorse around.

But there was another great horse that Seabiscuit had never raced. This horse's name was War Admiral. There was only one way to tell which horse was faster. The owners planned a race between the two horses.

Many people turned out for the race on November 1, 1938. All over the country, people listened to the race on the radio. When the bell rang, War Admiral and Seabiscuit began to run. Side by side, the two horses ran like the wind. Seabiscuit pulled ahead, but War Admiral caught up to him. The crowd roared.

Together, the horses headed for the finish line. Then Seabiscuit pulled ahead again. But this time War Admiral was too tired to catch up. Seabiscuit won the race by just a few yards!

Today, people think of the race between Seabiscuit and War Admiral as one of the greatest ever. Charles Howard and Tom Smith are famous, too. They gave a losing horse a second chance.

1. Why did Seabiscuit's first owner put him up for sale?

   Ⓐ He did not like horses anymore.

   Ⓑ He knew someone else could help Seabiscuit.

   Ⓒ He needed a way to get some money.

   Ⓓ He did not want to keep a horse that lost races.

2. What made Seabiscuit so tired and mean?

_____

_____

3. Seabiscuit began to calm down when _____.

   Ⓐ Charles Howard bought him

   Ⓑ he made friends with a goat

   Ⓒ Tom Smith put a friendly horse beside him

   Ⓓ he started racing other horses again

4. Why did Seabiscuit grow to like Tom Smith?

_____

_____

5. Why did Seabiscuit win the race?

_____

_____

Passage 23   Comparing and Contrasting

Animal Baths

To wash yourself, you take a bath or a shower. Animals need to keep clean, too. How do animals clean themselves?

Cats lick themselves to keep their fur clean. Have you ever watched a pet cat clean itself?

Elephants take baths much as you do. But instead of hopping into the tub, they walk into a river or lake.

Pigs also like to roll around in water. This keeps them clean and cool. If there is no clean water, they will roll in mud on a hot day. They do this to cool off. Pigs do not really like mud. They are happier in a nice, clean pond.

Bats have a funny way to groom. They lick their thumbs to clean their ears!

Guess how polar bears clean themselves. They use snow, of course! Some animals take baths in dust instead of water! The wombat is an Australian animal with lots of fur. To get clean, it lies down. Then it scoops sand all over itself!

Birds clean themselves in many ways. Sometimes they wash in water. That's why some people put birdbaths in their yard. At other times birds take dust baths, just like wombats. Birds also use their beaks to keep their feathers clean. They use their beaks the way you use a comb.

Sometimes a bird has itchy bugs in its feathers. Birds may use ants to help them clean off the bugs. A bird will lie down on an ant nest. Then the ants will crawl on the bird. The ants make a kind of bug spray on the feathers. Then the itchy bugs die!

Birds take baths in something else besides dust and ants! Some birds take "smoke baths." They sit on chimneys. They wave their wings in the smoke!

1. Name two animals that take dust baths.

_____

_____

2. What is a pig's favorite way to get clean?

ⓐ It takes a bath in clean water.

ⓑ It licks itself.

ⓒ It rolls in nice, thick mud.

ⓓ It lies down on ants.

3. How is a polar bear's bath different from a cat's bath?

_____

_____

4. A bird uses its beak like a person uses a _____.

ⓐ tub   ⓒ lake

ⓑ comb   ⓓ shower

5. How are the ways elephants and birds take baths alike? How are they different?

_____

_____

_____

Writing Prompt: Think about the way a pet or animal that you know takes a bath. How is it like and different from the way that people take baths?

Passage 24   Story Elements

Home Again

Niki saw the sign first. It said Welcome to Layton. "We're here!" Niki said.

"Yes," answered Mom. "Now I'll show you where I grew up."

Mom turned right and then left. "This is Norbeck Street. Let's find my old house." She stopped the car in front of a red house and said, "Oh, my!"

"What's wrong?" asked Niki.

"It's so *different* now," Mom said sadly. "The porch and the fence are gone." Mom became quiet. Then she said, "Let's see how Main Street looks."

As the car moved up Main Street, Mom and Niki looked from side to side. "Is Main Street the way you remember it?" Niki asked.

"No," Mom sighed. "Not much is the same." But then she smiled. "Look, Niki! The Layton Diner is still here!" Mom pulled the car into the parking lot. "Let's go in and get some lunch."

Niki and Mom walked into the diner. Mom looked around and laughed. "It hasn't changed a bit. Even the wallpaper is still the same!"

A waitress led Mom and Niki to their table. They sat down, and Mom looked at the menu. "Just like the old days!" said Mom.

Just then, a woman with white hair sat at the next table. The waitress said something and the woman laughed. Niki saw Mom's eyes grow wide. "What is it, Mom?" she asked.

"That laugh," Mom said softly. "I remember that laugh." She turned and looked at the woman. When she turned back, she said, "I don't know who that woman could be."

42

Niki looked past Mom and smiled at the woman. The woman smiled back kindly at Niki. Then the woman gasped with surprise. She stood up and walked over to Mom and Niki's table. She looked closely at Mom's face before she spoke. "Margaret, it's so nice to see you after all these years."

Mom gave the woman a blank look.

"I'm Mrs. Blade," the woman said. "Your third-grade teacher."

Mom jumped up and hugged Mrs. Blade. "I didn't know who you were."

Mrs. Blade laughed loudly again. "I didn't know who you were either, Margaret," she said. Then she turned toward Niki and said, "But your daughter looks just like you did in third grade. And I never forget a student's face."

1. What were Mom and Niki doing in this story?

_____

_____

2. How did Mom feel when she saw her old house?

Ⓐ sad   Ⓒ sleepy

Ⓑ happy   Ⓓ mad

3. Where did Mom and Niki stop for lunch?

_____

4. Why did Mom turn around and look at the woman with white hair?

_____

_____

5. Who was the woman with white hair?

Ⓐ Mom's school friend

Ⓑ Mom's third-grade teacher

Ⓒ a waitress at the diner

Ⓓ Niki's third-grade teacher

43

Passage 25   Making Inferences and Predictions

www.blairelementaryschool.net

WELCOME TO OUR WEB PAGE!

Blair Elementary School News for March

Special Dates: March 4 Mrs. Mohan's class takes a trip to North Park Zoo. The bus will leave school at 12:00 P.M. and come back at 3:00 P.M. Wear shoes that feel good.

March 16 School will end at 12:30 P.M.

March 30 This is School Picture Day. Wear a big smile to school!

Ways You Can Help:

- Do you have some extra yarn at home? Mr. King needs it! Drop the yarn in the box near the art room.
- Bring back the books! Mrs. Nolen says many students need to bring back school library books. She has sent out notes about missing books.
- Should Blair Elementary School have a science fair? Jan Lee thinks so. She wants to start one. But she needs other parents to help her. If you want to help, call Jan at 555-6791.

Other News:

- This spring, Mrs. Bain's class will be in charge of the school's flower garden near the front door.
- Laurie Burks visited Mr. Wayne's class. She sang some of her songs to the class. The class gave Laurie a big hand.

44

1. **Why do you think students should wear shoes that feel good on the zoo trip?**

   (A) They will be doing a lot of walking.

   (B) They will be riding on animals.

   (C) You need special shoes to go to the zoo.

   (D) Other kinds of shoes scare the zoo animals.

2. **What does "wear a big smile"on March 30 mean?**

   (A) Students should smile for their pictures.

   (B) Students should wear tags with smiles on them.

   (C) Students should wear clothes with smiles on them.

   (D) Students should always be happy in school.

3. **The flower garden will be near the "front door." What do you think the "front door" is?**

   (A) the front door of Mrs. Bain's class

   (B) the front door of the school

   (C) the front door of a student's house

   (D) the front door of a greenhouse

4. **Which of these people do you think works in the school library?**

   (A) Mr. Wayne

   (B) Mrs. Mohan

   (C) Laurie Burks

   (D) Mrs. Nolen

5. **Why do you think "the class gave Laurie a big hand"?**

   _____

   _____

Answer Key

1. Rabbit Laughs

1. C
2. Rabbit had to clear a field of weeds.
3. D

2. Here Comes the Sun

1. Paint the back of the plate yellow.
2. Cut out the 7 hands.
3. A

3. Troll's New Look

1. A
2. He has a lonely job and people don't smile at him.
3. He takes a bath, gets a haircut, and buys new clothes.
4. town
5. He feels sad and lonely at the beginning; he feels happy at the end.

4. Meet Jorge Estrella

1. A
2. D
3. at the building where he works
4. On an easy day, few things would happen. Jorge might write just a few stories.
5. A

5. Rules for Our School

1. A
2. C
3. Sample answer: Be nice to other people.
Writing Prompt: Answers will vary.

6. Talk With Your Hands

1. D
2. C
3. ball
4. dog
5. Answers should include two of the following: from a book, a friend, or a teacher.

7. The Right Pet

1. He was trying to catch a mouse.
2. D
3. C

8. Peanut Butter Fudge

1. C
2. B
3. Crush the peanuts with a rolling pin.
4. Take the bowl out and stir well.
5. Cool the pan for one hour.

9. The Snow Party

1. C
2. A
3. A
4. Sample answer: She was worried about letting go of the sled.
5. She rolled off the sled.

10. Frieda and Her Trick

1. Frieda lives in a zoo in Germany.
2. food
3. B

11. Creepy Spiders

1. She was afraid of spiders.
2. to help her get used to seeing spiders
3. D
4. Yes. She is now able to catch spiders even though she is still a little afraid of them.
5. Answers will vary. Students should mention a fear and a way of helping someone overcome it.

12. Asteroid Just Misses Boy!

1. D
2. The asteroid hit Earth hard.
3. It almost hit him.

13. Riding the Board

1. D
2. She put out her arm.
3. B
4. C
5. She showed the X-ray picture to Dad and Yoko.

14. The Clean-Up Team

1. C
2. B
3. Mr. Trent used to pick up the trash, but he moved away.
4. Mrs. Gill's back was stiff.
5. She wore Mrs. Gill's gardening gloves.

15. Sisters in Space

1. Venus is covered with thick clouds.
2. to learn more about the planet
3. D
4. C
5. Venus has plains, mountains, and valleys.

16. The Very Hungry Kid

1. morning
2. up a mountain to some grass
3. Sample answer: He thought there wasn't enough grass for him on the first mountain, and he thought he saw grass on the next mountain.
4. Instead of grass, he found weeds that tasted bad.
5. D

Writing Prompt: Answers will vary.

17. Snow Caves

1. B
2. Brush the snow off.
3. to keep your body heat in the cave

18. Mama's Magic Trick

1. Rosa, Anita, and Felipe came to the kitchen for dinner.
2. B
3. Mama came back to the kitchen, pointed the wand at the children, and told them to love the food.

19. What Is a Whale?

1. Both have fins.
2. A *school* is a group of fish; a *pod* is a group of whales.
3. A
4. D
5. Both have four parts.

20. What Did You Say?

1. B
2. C
3. A
4. go to sleep or go to bed
5. D

21. Bug Eaters

1. the sundew plant and the rainbow plant
2. B
3. the teasel

22. A Second Chance for Seabiscuit

1. D
2. His first owner had raced him too hard.
3. C
4. He was kind.
5. War Admiral was too tired to catch up.

23. Animal Baths

1. wombats and birds
2. A
3. A polar bear uses snow, but a cat licks itself.
4. B
5. Both elephants and birds take baths in water. Unlike elephants, birds also take baths in dust, ants, and smoke. They also use their beaks.
Writing Prompt: Answers will vary.

24. Home Again

1. They were visiting the town where Mom grew up.
2. A
3. the Layton Diner
4. Mom remembered the laugh, so she turned to see who was laughing.
5. B

25. Blair Elementary School News for March

1. A
2. A
3. B
4. D
5. It means the class clapped for Laurie because they liked her songs.